Step by Step

Rice

Step by Step
Rice

Anne Chapman

Bloomsbury Books
London

Page 2: Risotto with Asparagus makes an excellent lunch or first course. It is also a welcome sign of spring when the fragrant bunches begin appearing in the shops. The preparation for this dish is shown on the front and back endpapers.

This edition published in 1994 by
Bloomsbury Books
an imprint of
The Godfrey Cave Group
42 Bloomsbury Street, London. WC1B 3QJ
under license from
Harlaxton Publishing Limited

Harlaxton Publishing Limited
2 Avenue Road, Grantham, Lincolnshire, NG31 6TA
United Kingdom
A Member of the Weldon International Group of Companies

First Published in 1994

© Copyright 1994 Harlaxton Publishing Limited
© Copyright 1994 Design Harlaxton Publishing Limited

Publisher: Robin Burgess
Project Coordinator: Barbara Beckett
Designer: Rachel Rush
Editor: Alison Leach
Illustrator: Maggie Renvoize
Jacket Photographer: Rodney Weidland
Inside Photographer: Andrew Elton
Produced by Barbara Beckett Publishing
Colour Separation: G.A. Graphics, Stamford, UK
Printer: Imago, Singapore

British Library Cataloguing-in-Publication data.
A catalogue record for this book is available from the British Library

Title: Step by Step, RICE
ISBN: 1 85471 308 6

Step by Step

Contents

Cook's Notes

Measurements

As the metric/US equivalents given are not exact, follow only one system of measurement within the recipe. All spoon and cup measures are level and standard spoon and cup measurements are used in all the recipes. I recommend using a graduated nest of measuring cups: 1 cup, ½ cup, ⅓ cup and ¼ cup. The graduated nest of spoons comprises 1 tablespoon, 1 teaspoon, ½ teaspoon and ¼ teaspoon. For liquids, use a standard litre or imperial pint measuring jug, which also shows cup measurements.

Ovens should be preheated to the specified temperature. The heat on top of the cooker (stove) should be set at medium unless otherwise stated.

Note: When measuring rice it is more accurate to measure by cup rather than weight. Use the same cup for measuring the water or other liquid.

Ingredients

Fresh fruit and vegetables should be used in the recipes unless otherwise stated. **Herb** quantities are for fresh herbs; if fresh are unobtainable, use half the quantity of dried herbs. Use freshly ground black **pepper** whenever pepper is listed; use **salt** and pepper to individual taste. Use plain (all-purpose) **flour** unless otherwise stated. Fresh **ginger** should be used throughout, unless ground ginger is called for. Use fresh **chillies**; if substituting dried chillies, halve the quantity. Cold-pressed virgin olive **oil** is recommended, but any type may be used. Use unsalted **butter**. Preferably use fermented wine **vinegar**; however, cider vinegar and malt vinegar may be substituted if preferred. White granulated **sugar** is used unless stated otherwise. When buying **rice**, check the packet to see whether or not it should be washed.

English Baked Rice Pudding (p. 44), served here with cream and garnished with strawberries.
The smooth creamy texture appeals to young and old alike.

Introduction

Versatile rice can be eaten in hundreds of different ways. This soothing, fragrant grain can be flavoured to make a grand party dish such as Spanish paella (saffron rice with chicken and seafood), or pilau or pilaf rice can be an accompaniment to spicy curries or baked dishes. Rice can be the basis of a salad or a soup, or an Italian asparagus risotto. It can be stuffed into chickens and vegetables and even sweetened to make a baked rice pudding.

In a number of languages the word for rice is the same as the word for food, so people will ask each other 'Have you had rice?', meaning, 'Have you eaten?'. Rice is often the symbol of life and fertility, and is thrown at a bride and groom at weddings. Rice originated in the south of China and spread throughout Asia where it is the staple grain of most countries.

It is worth following some of the original methods of cooking rice before modern marketing stepped in. I recommend that you disregard the instructions on the package and instead use the well-tested methods for cooking rice given in this book. Rice is extremely easy to cook, so you do not need to buy quick-cooking, 'instant' rice, or parboiled rice or preseasoned rice.

Long-grain rice is used for most dishes such as pilaus and pilafs, soup and salads. When well cooked, the rice grains remain separated. Basmati rice is a special-tasting Indian rice which, though expensive, is worth using for festive occasions.

Short-grain rice is more glutinous and is used for stuffings or desserts or whenever the dish needs the rice to stick together. Glutinous rice is another variety that can be used for stuffing.

Arborio rice is the swollen, short-grain rice especially grown for risottos and sweet dishes.

Brown rice is the unhusked grain and is far better nutritionally—it just needs to be cooked an extra 10–20 minutes. You can use brown rice for any of these recipes.

Wild rice is not actually a rice as such but may be cooked the same way as brown rice. It is a fragrant and tasty rice particularly suited for stuffing poultry and game.

Read the package instructions to determine whether you need to wash the grains. A lot of the rice from India and Sri Lanka needs to be picked over for small stones as well. It is sometimes recommended to soak rice. If you do, add a little less liquid when cooking.

To make a rice dish more special, saffron is added to give it a beautiful yellow colour as well as flavour. Saffron is expensive and is used sparingly. It takes hundreds of the crocus flower stigmas to make even a teaspoonful of saffron.

An important part of rice cooking is to have a heavy cast iron pot with a well-fitting lid. The thick base will ensure even cooking and retention of heat. The rice boils as well as absorbs the steam while cooking, so it is important that no steam escapes. No other special equipment is needed except very sharp knives to cut fruit, vegetables and meats. A wok is excellent for large rice dishes like paella or biryani as well as stir-frying, of course. I always recommend buying a food processor because it saves so much time and energy.

The recipes in this book are drawn from cuisines all over the world: China, India, America,

Spain, Italy, France and the United Kingdom. There are recipes for pilau, pilaf and spicy rices; rice as soup and risotto; rice as a main meal; rice as stuffing for vegetables and meats; rice salads; and rice as dessert.

The instructions are clearly set out. There are step-by-step guides to different cooking methods such as the absorption method of cooking rice, baked rice puddings and risotto made on the top of the cooker. Many of the recipes are photographed in preparation stages to show special techniques as well as what the finished dish looks like and how to present it at the table. Detailed step-by-step drawings also illustrate special techniques such as rolling a sushi in a bamboo mat and jointing a chicken There are handy hints set in boxes giving information on how to clean mussels, prepare mayonnaise and make your own garam masala.

The recipes are cross-referenced within the book. For example, you can quickly refer to the basic recipe for cooking rice by the absorption method and how to prepare prawns (shrimp).

A glossary of cooking terms is on the last page for you to look up any term that is unfamiliar. There is a list of recipes (p. 5) for your reference. Be sure to read the information on measurements and ingredients (p. 6).

One of the most important things to do when trying a new recipe is to read the recipe very thoroughly before starting. Check that you have all the ingredients, and make an estimate of the amount of time needed.

I hope you discover the delights of cooking with rice, as one-third of the world already has. Be adventurous after mastering these recipes and begin to experiment with your own balance of flavourings. The world of cooking and tasting never ends—it can be an adventure you enjoy every day.

The preparation for Rice Pilaf (p. 11) shown with the rice and onion glistening with butter just before the water is added.

Accompaniments

Rice harmonizes particularly well with sauced dishes—it is such a delicious way to soak up those flavoursome sauces and juices. Follow the Absorption Method below, using any of its variations to make an excellent tasty pilaf. Sometimes a meal is made more flavoursome by making the rice itself spicier or adding extra flavours that will harmonize with other dishes. These recipes for pilafs, pilaus and spicy rices can be served as accompaniments or as dishes in themselves for a light meal.

Absorption Method of Cooking Rice

The aim of the 'absorption' method of cooking rice is to cook the rice in as little water as possible so the grains swell but remain separate. When well cooked, the rice should be tender but a little firm, and never mushy. Follow this chart carefully to avoid soggy rice!

Long-grain and short-grain rice: For 1 part rice use 1½ parts water.
Presoaked rice: For 1 part rice use 1⅓ parts water.
Brown rice: For 1 part rice use 2 parts water.
Note: 1 cup of rice makes 3 cups of cooked rice.
    The first secret of successful rice cooking is learning to measure the rice by volume (cup) rather than weight. When measuring rice use the same cup for the rice and the water.

1½ cups water   *Salt, if liked*
1 cup rice, washed if necessary

Bring the water to the boil, throw in the rice and salt. Stir once and when the water comes back to the boil, turn the heat down to the lowest temperature, cover with a tight-fitting lid and cook for 20 minutes. If you don't have a tight-fitting lid put a layer of foil between the saucepan and the lid to seal. Leave to stand for 10 minutes, covered, then fluff it up with a fork.

Variations
Use chicken stock (p. 21) instead of water.
Add 1 tablespoon of butter with the rice.
Add ¼ teaspoon of saffron threads, soaked, and 1 tablespoon of butter with the rice.
Add a few sliced mushrooms with the rice and use chicken stock (p. 21) instead of water.
Garnish the cooked rice with chopped spring onions (scallions).
Garnish with chives, chervil and stir in 1 tablespoon of butter.

Absorption Method of Cooking Rice

1½ cups of water and 1 cup of rice make 3 cups of cooked rice.   *Bring water to the boil, add rice and salt.*   *Bring back to the boil, then cover and simmer.*   *Rice is cooked after 20 minutes. Leave to stand for 10 minutes, covered, then fluff up with a fork.*

  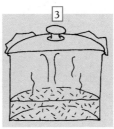 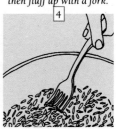

Rice Pilaf

This is a classic French way to make rice as an accompaniment to chicken, beef, veal or lamb dishes. Add ¼ teaspoon of saffron soaked in a little warm water if liked.

45 g/1½ oz/3 tablespoons butter
1 onion, chopped
1½ cups long-grain rice

3 cups water
Salt and pepper
Bouquet garni (see below)

Heat the butter in a saucepan and add the onion. Sauté until the onion is soft. Add the rice and stir for a few minutes, until all the rice grains are glistening with butter. Add the water, salt, pepper and bouquet garni and bring to the boil. Stir once, turn the heat down as low as possible and cover tightly. Cook for 20 minutes. Remove from heat. Leave to stand, covered, for 10 minutes, then lift the lid off and fluff up the rice with a fork.
Serves 6

Sherry Rice
Sherry Rice is a popular-flavoured pilaf from Spain. Follow the instructions above but replace the water with 2½ cups of chicken stock (p. 21) and 5 tablespoons of medium dry sherry. When cooked, sprinkle in 2 tablespoons of sherry just before leaving it to stand for 10 minutes. Fork through the grains and sprinkle over ¼ teaspoon of cayenne.
Serves 6

Bouquet Garni: *A combination of fresh bay leaf, thyme and parsley tied with string or, if dried, tied up in a muslin (cheesecloth) bag. Used to flavour soups, casseroles and braised dishes, stocks, poached and boiled dishes and sauces.*

Prawn Pilaf

A tasty pilaf from South Carolina. To make prawn (shrimp) stock from the prawn shells, simply pour cold water over the shells, add some peppercorns and a bouquet garni (p. 11) and boil for 45 minutes. Strain through a fine sieve (strainer).

1 tablespoon butter

3 rashers (slices) bacon, rinds removed, cut into dice

2 onions, chopped

3 tomatoes, chopped

3 chillies, chopped

1 tablespoon chopped ginger

2 cups long-grain rice

3 cups prawn (shrimp) stock

Salt and pepper

800 g/1¾ lb prepared prawns (shrimp), (see below)

3 tablespoons snipped chives, to garnish

Melt the butter in a pan and sauté the bacon and onions until the onions are soft. Add the tomatoes, chillies and ginger and sauté until the tomatoes are soft. Add the rice and cook for 2 minutes, stirring continuously. Pour in the prawn stock and bring to the boil. Add the salt and pepper, stir once and turn the heat to low. Cover tightly and cook for 15 minutes. Remove the lid and add the prawns. Stir with a fork. Replace the lid and leave to stand for 10 minutes. Serve garnished with chives.

Serves 8-10

Preparing Prawns (Shrimp)

Remove the head. | *Take off the shell and legs, leaving the tail intact.* | *Make a cut along the back.* | *Remove intestine with a toothpick or skewer. Wash thoroughly.*

Spicy Rice: *Aromatic rice dishes are popular all over Asia and the Middle East and the variations are seemingly endless. They go well with spicy meat and vegetable dishes or can be a meal in themselves, served with some yoghurt and pickles. Experiment with the spices and don't be afraid to add a tablespoon or two of nuts or peas, tomatoes or chopped spinach.*

Rice Pilaf (p. 11) shown here as an accompaniment to a grilled (broiled) chicken dish. Saffron threads, soaked in warm water, can be added for colour and flavour.

Spicy Pilau with Peas

2 tablespoons mustard seed oil or vegetable oil
3 whole cloves
8 peppercorns
1 cinnamon stick
8 cardamom pods
1 tablespoon coriander seeds

1 tablespoon cumin seeds
1½ cups long-grain or basmati rice
3 cups water
1 teaspoon turmeric
1 teaspoon salt, if liked
150 g/5 oz/1 cup shelled peas

Heat the oil in a pot and add all the spices except the turmeric. Stir until they begin to change colour. Add the rice and stir until all the grains are glistening. Add the water, turmeric and salt and bring to the boil. Turn the heat down low, add the peas, cover tightly and cook for 20 minutes. Leave to stand for 10 minutes, then fluff up with a fork.
Serves 6

The ingredients for Chinese Fried Rice, ready to be cooked quickly in the wok.

Chinese Fried Rice

The cooked rice for this dish should be broken up into individual grains.
Just wet your fingers and run them through the cold rice.

125 g/4 oz prepared prawns (shrimp), (p. 12)
¼ teaspoon salt
1 teaspoon cornflour (cornstarch)
2 teaspoons water
4 tablespoons oil
½ cup diced cooked chicken
75 g/2½ oz/½ cup diced cooked ham

75 g/2½ oz/½ cup shelled peas
125 g/4 oz/1 cup fresh bean sprouts
3 cups cooked long-grain rice (p. 10)
2 spring onions (scallions), chopped
1 tablespoon dry sherry
1 tablespoon light soy sauce

Depending on how big the prawns are, slice them in half lengthwise and cut into 6 mm/¼ inch pieces. Mix together the salt, cornflour and water, and coat the prawns with the mixture. Set aside for 30 minutes.

Heat the wok and then heat half the oil. Add the prawns and cook for a few minutes, stirring continuously. Remove the prawns with a slotted spoon. Clean the wok and reheat. Add the remaining oil, put in the chicken, ham, peas and prawns and stir-fry for 1 minute. Add the bean sprouts, rice, spring onions, sherry and soy sauce. Keep stirring for a few minutes until the rice is heated through. Spoon on to a warm serving dish.
Serves 6

Lemon Rice

Serve with grilled (broiled) lamb chops, veal cutlets or chicken pieces.

3 tablespoons oil

5 tablespoons black mustard seeds

2 cups cooked long-grain rice (p. 10)

Juice of 4 lemons

30 g/1 oz/⅓ cup desiccated (shredded) coconut

1 teaspoon turmeric

4 chillies, chopped

125 g/4 oz/1 cup chopped pistachio nuts

1 lemon, thinly sliced

Heat the wok, then heat the oil. Put in the mustard seeds and cook until they pop. Add the rice, lemon juice, coconut, turmeric and chillies. Keep stirring for about 5–10 minutes until the rice is heated through. Add the pistachios and lemon slices and cook for a few minutes, stirring continuously. Serve immediately.

Serves 4

Chinese Fried Rice, ready to be served and eaten.

Soups and Risottos

The basic ingredient for these delicious first-course or lunch dishes is a good chicken stock (p. 21). Of course nothing tastes as good as homemade, but you can buy preservative-free stocks in the supermarket these days which are excellent. The fresher your ingredients are, the better these soups and risottos will taste.

Try to buy arborio rice for the risotto—it was especially cultivated for these dishes. The wide-grained rice responds particularly well to slow cooking. If you cannot get it, use short-grain rice.

The Italians like to eat their rice *al dente*, that is, soft and creamy on the outside while remaining slightly firm in the middle.

When cooking risotto the onions and rice are coated with butter first so that the flavour of the butter will soak in before the stock is added.

The stock should always be kept simmering beside the risotto pot. Cold stock would interrupt and delay the cooking. It takes about 25 minutes to cook a risotto and it must be stirred continuously to prevent the rice from sticking. The stock is added gradually as it is absorbed by the rice. This may appear irksome but it is actually pleasant and relaxing to stir and breathe in the aromas from the pan. A risotto should still have some stock left but not be too wet. If you run out of liquid, add water to the risotto.

Freshly grated Parmesan cheese and butter are usually added at the end of the cooking time. Serve in warm, wide soup plates and offer extra Parmesan cheese if liked.

Rice and Celery Soup

A lovely beginning to a special meal. Make a soup when you haven't the time to spend making a risotto. Celery must be stringed before cooking. At the top of the stick you will see the strings protruding from the rest. With a small sharp knife pull each one away down the length of the stick. Several can be done at once.

3 tablespoons olive oil	1 cup arborio rice
4 sticks celery, cut into dice	2 cups chicken stock (p. 21)
1 onion, chopped	Salt and pepper
2 cups water	3 tablespoons grated Parmesan cheese
30 g/1 oz/2 tablespoons butter	2 tablespoons snipped chives, to garnish

Put the olive oil in a saucepan and heat. Add the celery and onion and sauté until they have softened. Add the water, cover and simmer until the celery is tender. Purée two-thirds of the celery and onion in a food processor together with all the liquid.

The ingredients for Spicy Rice Soup (p. 18), set out ready to be made into an aromatic meal.

Melt the butter in a saucepan and add the rice. Stir until the grains all glisten, then add the stock, celery and onion mixture and the puréed mixture. Bring to the boil. Add salt and pepper to taste. Simmer for 20 minutes until the rice is *al dente*. Add the Parmesan cheese and mix well. Serve garnished with chives.

Serves 4

Dicing an Onion

Peel onion and cut lenghwise into two halves, keeping root intact to hold it together.	*Place halves flat side down. Make lenghwise cuts, stopping short of root.*	*Carefully, make horizontally cuts towards the root, which is still intact.*	*Slice crosswise from top to root to obtain dice.*

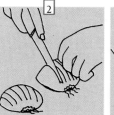
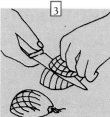

Garam Masala: *Mix together 1 tablespoon cardamom seeds, 1 tablespoon cumin seeds, 1 teaspoon cloves, 1 teaspoon peppercorns, 1 nutmeg and 1 cinnamon stick. Grind the spices together in a clean coffee grinder or food mill, or with a mortar and pestle. Store in an airtight tin.*

Spicy Rice Soup

A warming soup for the depths of winter. This recipe originates from the days of the British Raj in India. Add a chopped chilli and a bay leaf, if liked, when adding the garam masala.

60 g/2 oz/4 tablespoons butter	5¾ cups chicken stock (p. 21)
2 onions, chopped	1 teaspoon turmeric
1 tablespoon garam masala (see above)	Grated peel of 1 lemon
1 cup long-grain rice	½ cup coconut milk (see below)

Melt the butter in a saucepan and sauté the onions until they are soft. Add the garam masala and stir for 2 minutes. Add the rice and stir to coat the grains. Pour in the stock and turmeric and bring to the boil. Stir, cover and cook over the lowest heat for 20 minutes. Stir in the lemon peel and coconut milk and cook for a further few minutes.

Serves 4–6

Coconut Milk: *To make 350 ml/12 fl oz/1½ cups of coconut milk put 150 g/5 oz/3 cups of shredded coconut in a heatproof bowl and pour over 300 ml/½ pint/1¼ cups of boiling water. Leave to stand for 5 minutes, then strain. This is thick coconut milk. For thin coconut milk, repeat the process using the same coconut.*

Risotto with Wild Mushrooms

One of the most popular ways to enjoy an Italian risotto. This is a handy recipe to know as a quick meal can be made from your store cupboard (pantry) at a moment's notice.

20 g/¾ oz dried wild mushrooms (cepes or porcini)	2 tablespoons olive oil
4¼ cups chicken stock (p. 21)	2 cups arborio rice
1 onion, finely chopped	Salt and pepper
45 g/1½ oz/3 tablespoons butter	5 tablespoons grated Parmesan cheese

Spicy Rice Soup being dished up at the table, ready to eat. Serve with chapati or naan bread and garnish with mint or coriander (cilantro).

Wash the mushrooms quickly under running water, then soak them in 2 cups of warm water for 30 minutes. Strain them through a sieve (strainer) lined with paper towels. Set aside the mushrooms and retain the mushroom stock. Heat the chicken stock and keep it at a simmer.

Sauté the onion in 2 tablespoons of butter and the oil. When it is soft, add the rice and stir until all the grains glisten. Add some stock and stir for 15 minutes, then add the mushrooms, salt and pepper. Continue to cook for 10-15 minutes, adding chicken stock and the mushroom stock as the rice absorbs it. Add water if the rice begins to dry out and is not cooked.

When the rice is cooked to your liking, stir in the remaining butter and the Parmesan cheese.
Serves 6

Reconstituting Dried Mushrooms

| *Wash mushrooms under running water.* | *Soak in 2 cups of warm water for 30 minutes.* | *Strain the mushrooms through a sieve lined with paper towels.* | *Set aside the mushrooms and retain the mushroom stock.* |

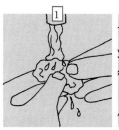 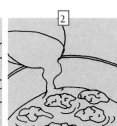 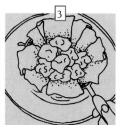 

Risotto with Asparagus

This risotto is richer with the addition of wine and cream. Make it when asparagus is in season. Don't attempt to make it with canned asparagus. The recipe comes from Venice and is known as Risotto con Asparagi.

450 g/1 lb asparagus	*½ cup dry white wine*
3¾ cups chicken stock (p. 21)	*2 tablespoons single (light) cream*
90 g/3 oz/6 tablespoons butter	*Salt and pepper*
1 onion, chopped	*5 tablespoons grated Parmesan cheese*
1 cup arborio rice	

Snap the asparagus off at the hard end where it naturally breaks. Cut into bite-sized pieces. Bring the stock to the boil and simmer. Heat half the butter in a saucepan. Add the onion and sauté until it is soft. Add the rice and stir until all the grains glisten. Add the wine and stir until it is nearly absorbed. Add half a cup of stock. Stir and continue to add stock for 15 minutes, then add the asparagus. When the rice is almost cooked, add the cream, salt and pepper. Keep stirring until *al dente,* then stir in the remaining butter and the Parmesan cheese.
Serves 4

Chicken Stock

1.25 kg/2¾ lb chicken bones and veal bones *2 celery sticks*
1 teaspoon peppercorns *Bouquet garni (p. 11)*
1 onion *1.4 litres/2½ pints/6¼ cups water*
1 carrot *1 teaspoon salt, if liked*

Put all the ingredients except the salt into a large saucepan. Make sure there is enough water to cover the bones. Bring to the boil slowly and keep skimming the surface to remove all the scum. Simmer gently for 3 hours. Add salt to taste. Strain the stock into a bowl and, when cool, chill. Remove the fat when it has set solid on the surface. Freeze if not required within 5 days.
Makes about 1 litre/1¾ pints/4 cups.

Tomato and Parma Ham Risotto

5 cups chicken stock (p. 21) *1½ cups arborio rice*
45 g/1½ oz/3 tablespoons butter *Salt and pepper*
1 onion, chopped *60 g/2 oz/½ cup grated Parmesan cheese*
90 g/3 oz Parma ham (prosciutto), cut into thin *500 g/18 oz tomatoes, peeled, seeded and cut into*
*   strips* *   9 mm/⅜ inch pieces*
2 tablespoons tomato paste *3 tablespoons chopped basil*

Tomato and Parma Ham Risotto shown about 10 minutes into cooking time.

This colourful Tomato and Parma Ham Risotto can be garnished with slivers of Parmesan when served. Accompany with a salad and a glass of wine.

Bring the chicken stock to the boil and simmer. Melt the butter and sauté the onion until it is tender. Add the ham and tomato paste and sauté for 2 minutes. Add the rice and stir for several minutes. Begin adding the chicken stock half a cup at a time, stirring continuously. Continue adding stock for 25 minutes or until the rice is nearly cooked. Add salt and pepper to taste. Stir in the Parmesan cheese, tomatoes and basil. Keep stirring until the dish has completely heated through.

Serves 4

Main Meals

I n these wonderful dishes, rice is used in a variety of ways, sometimes surrounding the meat, at other times acting as stuffing for vegetables and poultry. Whichever way, these recipes are equally tasty and all make for flavourful meals. They are generally time-consuming to prepare though, so save them for special occasions. If you have any leftover cooked rice from a pilaf or pilau, it can quickly be stuffed into some blanched vegetables and lightly cooked for a fast meal.

If you do not have a saucepan with a tight-fitting lid, cover the top of the pan with foil and then cover. Crunch the foil to seal the pan so that no steam escapes.

Rice stuffing adds wonderful flavours to meats and vegetables and helps keep them moist while making the dish go further.

Always leave room for the stuffing to expand while cooking. Precook the onion and garlic as this aids digestion. Only ever stuff poultry just before cooking, otherwise harmful bacteria may develop.

Lamb and Apricot Polo (p. 26) being assembled for the final cooking which will blend the flavours together.

Lamb and Apricot Polo

This sweet and aromatic dish originates in Persia (Iran). In the Middle East they are very fond of the taste of fruit with meats. Try this recipe to see how delicious it is.

120 g/4 oz/½ cup butter
1½ onions, chopped
3 garlic cloves, chopped
500 g/18 oz/4 cups lamb cut into cubes
Salt and pepper
1 teaspoon ground cumin
1 teaspoon ground cinnamon

2 tablespoons raisins
100 g/3½ oz dried apricots, halved
1½ cups water
2 cups long-grain rice
5 cups water
½ teaspoon saffron threads, soaked in 2 teaspoons warm water

Heat half the butter in a saucepan and sauté the onions and garlic until soft. Add the meat and brown all over. Add the salt and pepper, cumin and cinnamon and mix well. Add the raisins and apricots and cover with water. Simmer, covered, for 1½ hours until the meat is tender. Reduce the sauce at the end if it is too liquid.

Cook the rice by the absorption method (p. 10), adding the remaining butter and the saffron.

In a large saucepan combine the rice and the meat in alternate layers, ending with rice. Pour in any leftover sauce. Cover tightly and cook over a low heat for another 20 minutes or until the sauce is absorbed by the rice.

Serves 4-6

Chicken Biryani

MARINADE
3 onions, chopped
3 garlic cloves, chopped
1 tablespoon chopped ginger
½ teaspoon ground cloves
1 tablespoon ground cardamom
1 tablespoon ground pepper
1 tablespoon ground coriander
1 tablespoon ground cinnamon
1 teaspoon salt
Juice of 2 lemons

275 ml/9 fl oz/1¼ cups yoghurt
2 tablespoons oil

1 chicken, jointed, skin removed if liked (p. 28)
2 cups long-grain or basmati rice
5 cups water
5 cardamom pods
1 teaspoon saffron threads, soaked in 2 teaspoons warm water
2 tablespoons milk

Overleaf: Some of the many varieties of rice. From the left: long-grain brown rice, wild rice, short-grain rice, short-grain brown rice, basmati rice, arborio rice and long-grain rice.

Right: I always admire the colourful textures of Lamb and Apricot Polo.

Jointing a Chicken

Cut off the legs at the point where the thigh bones join the body.

Slide a knife inside chicken and cut down each side of the backbone. Remove backbone.

Cut the wings off with a small portion of the breast.

There are now six pieces.

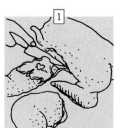 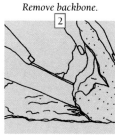 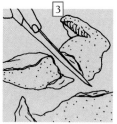 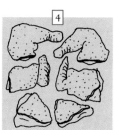

Place all the marinade ingredients in a food processor and blend to a paste. Put into a bowl and coat the chicken pieces liberally with the marinade. Cover and leave to rest for 2 hours at room temperature.

Place the chicken and marinade in a large saucepan. Bring to the boil and simmer for 15 minutes. Remove the chicken pieces with a slotted spoon and place in a casserole dish. Keep in a warm place. Reduce the liquid and spoon over the chicken.

In the meantime cook the rice by the absorption method (p. 10), adding the cardamom pods and saffron after the rice has come to the boil. Only cook the rice for 10 minutes, not 20 minutes. Drain the rice and place it on top of the chicken in the casserole. Sprinkle the milk over it. Cover the lid securely so no steam escapes. Bake in a preheated oven at 150°C/300°F/gas 2 for 1 hour. Serve garnished with thinly sliced fried onions, if liked.
Serves 6

Cleaning Mussels. *Soak the shells in fresh water and scrub to rid them of grit and seaweed. Trim the beards with a sharp knife. Discard any shells that are broken or open. Rinse thoroughly in cold water again.*

Making Paella

Sauté the onion, then the chicken until golden brown.

Sauté squid, fish and garlic.

Add the rice and stir well.

Pour in ⅓ of the stock and the vegetables, spices and remaining seafood.

Paella

A rich, fragrant rice dish from Spain originally cooked outdoors in a large, shallow pan over charcoal, similar to our barbecues. Traditionally it is made from a mixture of chicken and seafood but most often it is made in Spain from the fruits of the local countryside. If you don't have a paella pan, use a wide, shallow pan or a wok.

4 tablespoons olive oil
2 onions, chopped
½ chicken, jointed (p.28)
250 g/9 oz squid, cut into rings
800 g/1¾ lb white fish fillets, cut into bite-sized
    pieces
3 garlic cloves, chopped
2½ cups arborio rice
5 cups hot chicken stock (p. 21)
1 pepper (capsicum, bell pepper), seeded and
    cut into strips

24 French (green) beans, halved
150 g/5 oz/1 cup shelled peas
12 teaspoon saffron threads, soaked in 2
    teaspoons warm water
2 teaspoons paprika
Salt and pepper
300 g/11 oz prepared prawns (shrimp), (p. 12)
500 g/18 oz mussels, cleaned (p.28)
3 tomatoes, peeled and chopped
Bouquet garni (p. 11)
Lemon slices, to garnish

In a large pan heat the oil and sauté the onions until they are soft. Sauté the chicken in the same oil until golden brown. Add the squid and sauté for 5 minutes. Add the fish and garlic and seal the pieces. Add the rice and stir well. Pour in one-third of the stock and add the pepper, beans, and peas, saffron, paprika, salt and pepper along with the prawns and mussels. Stir the rice and make sure the ingredients are evenly distributed.

Pour in another third of the stock along with the tomatoes and bouquet garni. Cook for a further 10 minutes, then add the remaining stock. Continue to cook until the rice is cooked. Remove from heat, cover well and leave to stand for 10 minutes. Stir and serve on warm plates. Garnish with lemon slices.

Serves 6-8

Chicken with Rice and Mushroom Stuffing

STUFFING
15 g/½ oz/1 tablespoon butter
1½ rashers (slices) bacon, rinds removed, cut into dice
1 onion, chopped
125 g/4 oz/1 cup mushrooms, sliced
Salt and pepper
3 tablespoons Madeira
1½ cups cooked short-grain rice (p. 10)
1 egg

1 tablespoon chopped thyme

1 chicken
45 g/1½ oz/3 tablespoons butter
Juice of 1 lemon
1 teaspoon pepper
1½ cups chicken stock (p. 21)
1 cup white wine

To make the stuffing, melt the butter and add the bacon and onion. Sauté until the onion is soft, then add the mushrooms. Season with salt and pepper. Cook for a few minutes, then pour in the Madeira. Boil until almost dissolved and pour the contents of the pan into a bowl which contains the rice. Stir well and mix in the egg and thyme.

Trim the chicken and stuff the cavity. Fasten the opening with a small skewer. Rub the butter and lemon juice all over the skin and sprinkle with the pepper. Put the chicken, breast side up, on a rack in a roasting pan and pour the chicken stock into the pan. Place in a preheated oven at 220°C/425°F/gas 7. Baste every 15 minutes with the stock in the pan. After 20 minutes reduce the heat to 200°C/400°F/gas 6. Add water to the stock if it begins to dry up. The chicken should be ready in 1¼ hours or when the juice runs clear and not pink when pricked with a skewer in the thick part of the thigh. Season with salt. Transfer the chicken to a warm place.
Serves 4-6

Wine Sauce
Sop up the fat from the top of the stock with paper towels or spoon it off. Put the roasting pan on a high heat, add the wine and reduce the sauce to about half. Strain into a sauceboat.

Rice and Mushroom Stuffing

Wipe with a damp cloth. Cut ends off the stalks.   *Slice mushrooms vertically.*   *Prepare stuffing mixture and stuff the cavity of chicken just before cooking.*   *Close up the cavity with a small skewer.*

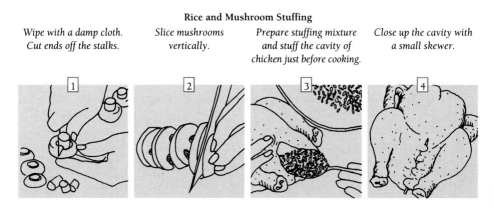

Stuffed Vine Leaves

A recipe from the Middle East. Use the same stuffing mixture as Stuffed Peppers(p. 33) to make these delectable little parcels to serve with drinks or as a snack. If you use fresh vine leaves, blanch them before using them and drain(p. 48). Preserved vine leaves should be washed and drained to get rid of the salt.

Lay a vine leaf flat on a board. Place 1 teaspoon of the rice mixture on the centre of the vine leaf. Fold the long ends of the leaf into the centre, then roll up the leaf to make an oblong package. Pack the packages into a wide-based pan, side by side so they won't be dislodged. Cover with water and sprinkle with the juice of a lemon. Simmer for 1 hour.

Spiced Apricot and Pine Nut Stuffing

Use this to stuff duck, chicken or a pocket in a boned leg of lamb. It is just as tasty as a stuffing for sweet peppers (capsicum, bell peppers), tomatoes and courgettes (baby marrows, zucchini).

2 tablespoons oil
1 onion, chopped
2 teaspoons garam masala (p.18)
1 tablespoon chopped ginger
Pinch of cayenne pepper
1 tablespoon tomato paste
2 cups cooked short-grain rice (p. 10)

3 tablespoons chopped coriander (cilantro)
1 tablespoon raisins
2 tablespoons chopped dried apricots
3 tablespoons pine nuts
Salt and pepper
Juice of 1 lemon

Heat the oil, add the onion and sauté until softened. Add the garam masala, ginger, cayenne and tomato paste, and sauté for a few minutes. Add the rice and the remaining ingredients and cook until everything is heated through. Remove from heat.

Stuffing vegetables and meats can be a most pleasurable aromatic task. Here, Stuffed Peppers (p. 33) are being assembled.

Stuffed Peppers

These tasty vegetables can be a meal in themselves or served individually as a starter or an accompaniment to a main meal. Use the same recipe for stuffing courgettes (baby marrows, zucchini). Blanch the vegetables for 3 minutes (p. 48) before stuffing them. Vegetables are eaten this way throughout the Mediterranean and Middle Eastern countries.

4 peppers (capsicums, bell peppers)
1 onion, chopped
3 tablespoons olive oil
250 g/9 oz/1¾ cups chopped cooked meat or chicken
1 tomato, peeled and chopped
2 tablespoons chopped olives

1 cup cooked short-grain rice (p. 10)
1 tablespoon chopped parsley
1 tablespoon chopped thyme
Salt and pepper
5 tablespoons grated Cheddar cheese

Cut the peppers in half lengthwise and remove the seeds and cores. Blanch them. Sauté the onion in oil until it softens, then add the meat and sauté for 2 minutes. Add the remaining ingredients except for the cheese. Stir well until the ingredients are heated through.

Stuff the peppers with the rice mixture and top with the grated cheese. Place them in a lightly oiled ovenproof dish and cook in a preheated oven at 180°C/350°F/gas 4 for about 25 minutes until nice and hot and the cheese has browned.

Serves 4

Stuffing Peppers (Capsicums, Bell Peppers)

| Cut the peppers in half lengthwise. | Remove cores and seeds. | Make the stuffing mixture and spoon into cavity of peppers. | Place peppers on an oiled ovenproof dish and top with grated cheese. |

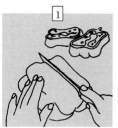 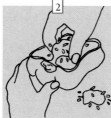 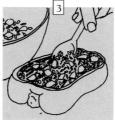 

Whether you serve Stuffed Peppers(capsicums, bell peppers) as a starter for a dinner party for 8 or as a main meal, they are bound to be very popular. They can also be prepared hours in advance. Leave the cooking until nearer eating time.

Trout with Wild Rice

The creamy sorrel sauce that goes with this dish is lemony and a bit sharp which contrasts with the rich cream. Sorrel is considered either a vegetable or a herb. If you cannot get it, use watercress instead. Only use the young fresh leaves and remove stalks.

30 g/1 oz/2 tablespoons butter
½ onion, chopped
1 garlic clove, chopped
½ cup wild rice
1¼ cups water
Salt and pepper
½ apple, cut into fine dice
2 egg yolks
3 tablespoons cream

4 x 300g/11 oz whole trout, washed and dried
SAUCE
30 g/1 oz/2 tablespoons butter
½ cup shredded sorrel leaves
5 tablespoons dry vermouth
2 tablespoons cream
Salt and pepper

8 baby sorrel leaves, to garnish

Melt the butter and sauté the onion and garlic until soft. Add the wild rice and stir for several minutes until all the grains glisten. Add the water, salt and pepper. Bring to the boil, then reduce the heat, cover and simmer for 20 minutes. Remove the lid and stir in the apple. Cook for another 5 minutes. Turn off the heat.

Blend the egg yolks together with the cream. Pour into the wild rice and allow to cook, covered, for a further few minutes in its own heat.

Let the mixture cool a little, then stuff it into the cavity of the trout. Brush oil onto some foil and securely wrap up each fish in a neat parcel. Place the fish in an ovenproof dish. Pour in some hot water so that it comes halfway up the fish parcels. Bake in a preheated oven at 220°C/425°F/gas 7 for 15 minutes.

Meanwhile, make the sauce. Melt the butter in a pan and add the sorrel. Keep cooking until it is limp, then add the vermouth and simmer until it has reduced by half. Pour in the cream and simmer until it thickens. Add salt and pepper to taste.

Unwrap the trout carefully and lay on warm plates. Pour the sauce over it. Garnish with baby sorrel leaves.

Serves 4

Wild Rice and Mushrooms

3 tablespoons lentils
2 cups hot water
1 cup wild rice
1½ cups water
30 g/1 oz/2 tablespoons butter
1 onion, finely chopped

3 garlic cloves, finely chopped
1 teaspoon chopped thyme
Pepper
24 button mushrooms, halved
4 tablespoons chopped parsley, to garnish

Put the lentils and hot water into a saucepan and simmer for about 20 minutes or until the lentils are just cooked. Drain.

At the same time put the wild rice and water into a saucepan and bring to the boil. Stir and turn down the heat to simmer. Cover and cook for 30 minutes.

Melt the butter in a saucepan and sauté the onion and garlic. Add the thyme, pepper and mushrooms and cook for 5 minutes. Add the wild rice and lentils and stir until they are heated through. Garnish with parsley.

Serves 6

Tomato and Spinach Rice

A wonderful rice dish to eat for lunch or a light meal accompanied by yoghurt and a chutney or pickle. It can be reheated most successfully.

3 tablespoons oil	1 teaspoon coriander seeds
1 onion, chopped	1 teaspoon cumin seeds
2 cups long-grain rice, washed	1 teaspoon cardamom pods
275 g/10 oz spinach leaves, cooked and finely chopped	2 teaspoons pepper
	3 cloves
2 tomatoes, finely chopped	Salt to taste
1 teaspoon turmeric	5 cups water

Heat the oil in the saucepan and sauté the onion until browned. Add the rice and stir for several minutes. Put in the spinach, tomatoes and spices. Stir and mix well together. Add the water and bring to the boil. Stir once, cover and simmer for 25 minutes. Leave to stand for 10 minutes before serving.

Serves 6

Rice and Chicken Mould

A lovely dish for a party since all the hard work can be done beforehand. If you don't want to go to the trouble of a mould, just put the rice in a bowl, mix through the chicken and sprinkle with slivered almonds and spices.

30 g/1 oz/2 tablespoons butter	1 chicken, cooked
1 onion, chopped	60 g/2 oz/½ cup pine nuts, roasted
2 cups rice	125 g/4 oz/1 cup slivered almonds, roasted
1 teaspoon salt	2 teaspoons ground cinnamon
90 g/3 oz/½ cup sultanas (golden raisins)	2 teaspoons ground cummin
750 ml/1¼ pints/3 cups chicken stock (p. 21)	2 teaspoons pepper

Melt the butter and sauté the rice until it is soft. Add the rice, salt and sultanas and stir for a few minutes. Add the stock, bring to the boil, then cover and simmer for 25 minutes. Remove from the heat and leave to stand for 10 minutes.

Meanwhile, remove all the flesh from the chicken, gently shredding it into fairly large pieces. Discard the skin and bones. Oil the mould. Place the pine nuts and almonds in the bottom of the mould and sprinkle with half of the spices. Pack the chicken pieces around the sides of the mould and fill the rest with the rice, sprinkling through the remaining spices. Press the ingredients firmly into the mould, then place a plate over it. Invert it onto the plate and very carefully remove the mould.

Serves 8

Stuffed Tomatoes with Basil

4 large firm tomatoes	*1¼ cups water*
3 tablespoons olive oil	*125 g/4 oz/¾ cup shelled peas*
1 onion, chopped	*1 egg*
2 garlic cloves, chopped	*3 tablespoons chopped basil*
½ cup short-grain rice	*Salt and pepper*

Slice off the top of the tomatoes and reserve as a lid. Carefully scoop out the seeds and pulp leaving a firm shell. Reserve the pulp. Sprinkle the shells with salt and leave them upside down to drain on a plate.

Heat 2 tablespoons of the oil in a pan and sauté the onion until tender. Add the garlic and stir for a minute. Then stir in the rice and keep stirring until all the rice grains glisten. Pour in the water and tomato pulp. Stir and bring to the boil. Stir once, cover tightly and turn the heat to low. Cook for 15 minutes. Stir in the peas.

In a bowl beat the egg lightly and stir in the rice mixture. Add the basil, and salt and pepper to taste. Stuff the mixture into the tomatoes and put the lids back on. Pack the tomatoes into an oiled ovenproof dish and sprinkle the rest of the oil over them. Bake them in a preheated oven at 180°C/350°F/gas 4 for about 35 minutes.

Serves 4

Peeling Tomatoes

Cut a small cross on each tomato.	*Put into a bowl and pour boiling water over them.*	*Peel the skin away from the cross area.*	*Slice or dice according to recipe.*

Step by Step

Salads

Rice makes the most delectable salads. The absorption method (p. 10) is the best way to cook the rice.

After the rice has cooked and rested, spread it out on paper towels to dry. If necessary, separate the grains with wet fingers before folding the rice in with the other ingredients.

Rice salad looks more attractive if served over a bed of lettuce leaves or garnished with some of the ingredients.

Spanish Prawn Salad (p. 38) in preparation. This is the best part of the cooking—when everything is assembled ready to be combined into a glorious salad to share with friends.

Spanish Prawn Salad

The Spanish love to flavour their rice with saffron, which always makes a dish look extra special.
Two cups of rice make 6 cups of cooked rice. Cook the soaked saffron with the rice.

2 cups long-grain rice
3 cups water
½ teaspoon saffron threads, soaked in 2 teaspoons
   warm water
150 g/5 oz/1 cup black olives, stoned (pitted)
500 g/18 oz cooked prawns (shrimp)
3 red peppers (capsicums, bell peppers), cut
   into strips
3 tomatoes, peeled and diced

DRESSING
4 tablespoons olive oil
1 tablespoon lemon juice
Grated peel of ½ lemon
Salt and pepper
2 tablespoons chopped basil or parsley

Lettuce leaves for serving

Cook the rice by the absorption method (p. 10) with the saffron. Spread out to cool. Put all the salad ingredients into a bowl and mix well. Combine the dressing ingredients in a screw-topped jar and shake well. Pour the dressing over the salad and mix gently.

Serve on a bed of tender lettuce leaves. If liked, reserve some of the strips of pepper, olives and prawns to garnish the rice.

Serves 4-6

Mayonnaise
2 egg yolks, at room temperature
1 teaspoon French mustard
¼ teaspoon salt

250 ml/8 fl oz/1 cup olive oil
1 tablespoon lemon juice

Beat together the egg yolks, mustard and salt. Add the oil, drop by drop, beating continuously. You can use a whisk, an electric beater or a food processor. As the mayonnaise thickens, you can add the oil in larger quantities. If the mayonnaise curdles, put a fresh egg yolk in a clean bowl and start again, dripping the curdled mayonnaise in drop by drop. When thick, add the lemon juice and stir in with a wooden spoon. You may need to add more lemon juice or hot water after it has been stored for a while, as it will thicken up again. Keeps for 2 weeks in the refrigerator.
Makes 250 ml/8 fl oz/1 cup.

It would be hard to match Spanish Prawn Salad for flamboyant colour.
The baby basil leaves make an appealing garnish. This salad makes an appetizing dish for lunch in the garden on a hot summer's day. Serve with iced, minted water as well as white wine.

Mediterranean Rice Salad

This salad is so rich it is a meal in itself.
The rice is moulded on a serving dish and garnished with slices of cucumber, tomato wedges, olives and watercress.

6 cups cooked long-grain rice (p. 10)
1 cucumber, ½ cut into dice, ½ thinly sliced
6 tomatoes, 4 cut into dice, 2 cut into wedges
1 red pepper (capsicum, bell pepper),
    cut into dice
2 chillies, chopped
2 onions, finely chopped
1 garlic clove, chopped
2 tablespoons capers

8 anchovy fillets
200 g/7 oz canned tuna
Salt and pepper
3 tablespoons olive oil
1 tablespoon lemon juice
125 ml/4 fl oz/½ cup mayonnaise (p. 38)
1 bunch watercress
3 tablespoons olives, stoned (pitted)

In a bowl combine the rice, diced cucumber, diced tomato, pepper, chillies, onions, garlic, capers, anchovy and tuna. Season with salt and pepper. Sprinkle with olive oil and lemon juice. Now mix in the mayonnaise. Transfer this mixture to a serving plate leaving plenty of room around the edge. With wet fingers, work the rice into a smooth mould. Clean the edge of the plate and surround the rice with plenty of watercress sprigs. Garnish the mould with the cucumber slices, tomato wedges and olives.

Serves 6-8

Brown Rice and Herb Salad

A delicious summer salad for lunch in the garden.

1 onion, chopped
4 tablespoons olive oil
1 garlic clove, chopped
2 teaspoons garam masala (p. 18)
¾ cup long-grain brown rice
1½ cups water
2 tablespoons desiccated (shredded) coconut

2 tablespoons raisins
2 tablespoons wine vinegar
Salt and pepper
2 tablespoons chopped coriander (cilantro)
2 tablespoons chopped mint
2 tablespoons slivered almonds

Sauté the onion in 1 tablespoon of the oil until softened. Add the garlic, garam masala and rice and stir for another few minutes. Add the water, coconut and raisins, and bring to the boil. Stir once, cover tightly and turn the heat down. Cook for 35 minutes or until just tender. Leave to stand for 10 minutes. Mix the remaining oil with the vinegar, salt and pepper and pour over the rice. Let the rice cool and just before serving mix through the coriander, mint and almonds.

Serves 4

Rolling Sushi

Place a sheet of nori on the mat near the end closest to you and place rice on it.	Spread the rice, add wasabi and tuna. Pick up bamboo mat and roll it tightly to compact rice.	Roll the mat up twice.	Unroll and cut the sushi into 6 pieces with a sharp knife.

   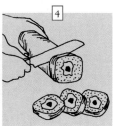

Rolled Sushi

Sushi is a popular Japanese way of serving raw seafood on vinegar-flavoured rice. Rolled sushi is made by rolling sheets of nori (dried seaweed sheets) around a rice roll with ingredients in the centre. Short-grain rice is used because it is glutinous and the grains will stick together. Fillings may include most kinds of raw seafood, sweet omelette and cucumber. Wasabi has the searing quality of mustard or horseradish and is used to heighten the flavours of bland food. It is most often available in dried or paste form. Simply mix the dried wasabi with a little water just before using.

1¾ cups short-grain rice
2¼ cups water
3 tablespoons rice vinegar or dry sherry
2 tablespoons sugar
¼ teaspoon salt

4 nori seaweed sheets
15 g/½ oz wasabi
175 g/6 oz very fresh tuna, cut into strips
2 tablespoons soy sauce

Cook the rice by the absorption method (p. 10). When it is cooked add the vinegar, sugar and salt and stir well. Cover and leave the rice to stand for 10 minutes. Uncover and let cool.

You need a bamboo mat or a piece of cardboard soft enough to roll up. Place a sheet of nori on the mat near the end closest to you. Place a handful of rice on it and spread the rice evenly over the nori leaving 21 mm/⅞ inch space all around so the rice won't spill out. Mix the wasabi with a little warm water to make a paste. Spread a little along the length of the rice. Put one-quarter of the tuna strips on top. Pick up the bamboo mat at the edge closest to you and roll it tightly from front to back to help compact the rice. Now roll the mat up again. Unroll and you have a long roll. Cut carefully with a heavy sharp knife into 6 pieces. Repeat the process. Serve with soy sauce for dipping. Add a little wasabi to the soy if you would like a bit more bite to the sauce.

Serves 4-6

Rice and Tuna Salad

A pleasure to the eye with the pale yellow rice, black olives, green peas and red peppers. Serve at room temperature for the tastiest flavour.

125 g/4 oz/⅔ cup pitted prunes
250 ml/8 fl oz/1 cup tea made with one teabag
200 g/7 oz canned tuna
3 cups cooked saffron rice (p. 10)
60 g/2 oz/⅓ cup chopped black olives
30 g/1 oz/¼ cup chopped almonds
150 g/5 oz/1 cup cooked peas

4 spring onions (scallions), sliced
½ cup mayonnaise (p. 38)
Juice of 1 lemon
Salt and pepper
1 red pepper (capsicum, bell pepper), cut into 12 mm/
⅝ inch strips, to garnish

Soak the prunes in tea for 2 hours; drain. Break up the tuna into bite-sized pieces. Combine prunes, tuna, rice, olives, almonds, peas, spring onions and mayonnaise in a large salad bowl. Add the lemon juice and salt and pepper to taste. Garnish with the red pepper.
Serves 6

Brown Rice and Corn Salad

This salad is deliciously crunchy and ideal to serve at a barbecue or picnic. It goes well with steak, chops and sausages.

6 cups cooked long-grain brown rice (p. 10)
150 g/5 oz/1 cup cooked corn kernels
3 celery sticks, sliced
6 spring onions (scallions), sliced
18 green olives, pitted and sliced
2 tablespoons parsley

VINAIGRETTE
1 tablespoon French (Dijon) mustard
Salt and pepper
Juice of ½ lemon
4 tablespoons olive oil

When the rice and corn are cool, combine them with the remaining vegetables and parsley in a salad bowl. Mix the vinaigrette ingredients together in a screw–topped jar, shake well and gently mix through the salad. Serve at room temperature.
Serves 6

White Rice: *To keep rice white when cooking in hard water, add a tablespoon of wine vinegar or a teaspoon of lemon juice to the water.*

Step by Step

Desserts

Short-grain rice makes wonderful desserts—homely and comforting dishes like baked rice pudding, or more sophisticated ones such as an Almond and Apricot Cake. Never wash the rice or you will remove the starch which is needed to keep the rice glutinous and sticking together.

Vanilla sugar is made by inserting a vanilla pod (bean) in a screw-topped jar of granulated sugar or caster (superfine) sugar. The pod soon flavours the sugar so keep your jar topped up.

Skimmed milk powder is excellent to use for rice puddings for a change.

Apple and Rice Pudding

The sweetness of the apples combined with the creamy rice results in a delightful, easy-to-make dessert. It can be prepared before your guests arrive and then popped in the oven.

1½ cups short-grain or arborio rice

3 tablespoons vanilla sugar, see above

3¾ cups milk

4 apples, peeled and chopped

30 g/1 oz/2 tablespoons butter

½ teaspoon ground cinnamon

Grated peel of ½ lemon

Simmer the rice and half the sugar in the milk until the rice is almost cooked. At the same time put the apples and remaining sugar into a saucepan with the butter, cinnamon and lemon peel and just cover with water. Simmer until the apples are cooked, then purée in a food processor.

Butter a pie dish and arrange alternate layers of rice and apples, finishing with rice. Bake in a preheated oven at 180°C/350°F/gas 4 for about 1 hour or until it is brown.

Serves 6

Saffron: *Red–gold stigmas from the crocus, hand-gathered and dried. Its flavour and yellow colour are used in Spanish, French, Italian and Indian cuisines. Soak 1/4 teaspoon of saffron threads in 2 teaspoons of warm water or milk before using. Saffron powder is available but it only gives the colour and not the flavour. Good saffron should be not more than a year old and a brilliant red and gold colour. It has a strong perfume with a pungent, bitter but pleasant taste. It will expand and colour immediately in hot water.*

Only a few simple ingredients make up English Baked Rice Pudding. Here, the pie dish is buttered, the lemon peel prepared—awaiting the rice, milk, cream, sugar and nutmeg.

English Baked Rice Pudding

This used to be one of our favourite puddings in winter when we were young. It was put into the oven to cook while the Sunday casserole or stew was still cooking in a slow oven.

5 cups milk
2 tablespoons single (light) cream
1 cup short-grain rice

30 g/1 oz vanilla sugar (p. 43)
Grated peel of ½ lemon
½ teaspoon grated nutmeg

Heat the milk and cream but do not boil. Butter a 1 litre/1¾ pint pie dish. Mix the rice with the milk and pour into the pie dish. Leave it to stand for 20 minutes. Stir in the sugar and lemon peel and sprinkle the top with nutmeg. Bake in a preheated oven at 150°C/300°F/gas 2 for 2 hours. Stir well every half an hour.

Serves 4

Sweet Saffron Rice

A sweet and spicy dessert from India. It can be made quickly with ingredients from your store cupboard (pantry), so keep it in mind for those days when you think you have nothing for dessert.

¾ cup short-grain rice
30 g/1 oz/2 tablespoons butter
5 cardamom pods
1 bay leaf
1 cup milk
2 tablespoons sugar

2 tablespoons single (light) cream
½ teaspoon saffron threads, soaked in 2 teaspoons
  warm water
2 tablespoons sultanas (golden raisins)
60 g/2 oz/½ cup chopped cashew nuts

Cook the rice in boiling water for 5 minutes and then drain. Melt the butter in a saucepan and sauté the rice, cardamom and bay leaf until they glisten, and then add the milk and sugar. Bring to the boil, stir once, lower the heat and cover tightly. Simmer for 15 minutes. Add the cream, saffron and sultanas, stir and leave to stand for 10 minutes, covered. Serve sprinkled with cashew nuts.

Serves 4

Caramel Rice Pudding

A very old-fashioned pudding that is easy to make though it may appear a little difficult at first. The taste is worth the effort! It will become a favourite I'm sure. You will need a straight-sided charlotte mould or baking dish.

1 cup long-grain rice
150 ml/1/4 pint/⅔ cup hot milk
225 g/8 oz/1 cup sugar
1 tablespoon grated lemon peel
60 g/2 oz/⅓ cup sultanas (golden raisins), soaked
  in hot water

90 g/3 oz/½ cup citrus peel
4 egg yolks
4 egg whites, stiffly beaten
60 g/2 oz/¼ cup sugar, extra
2 teaspoons water

Cook the rice in the milk in a saucepan for 15 minutes over a very low heat. Add the sugar, lemon, sultanas, and citrus peel. Remove from the heat. Stir in the egg yolks and gently fold in the egg whites.

Heat the extra sugar and the water in a charlotte mould. When the sugar has melted and turned light brown, tilt the mould so that the syrup coats the bottom and sides. Spoon the rice mixture into the mould and place the mould in a baking dish of hot water. Bake in a preheated oven at 180°C/350°F/gas 4 for 30 minutes. Unmould when cool. Serve with cream, mascarpone or melted jam.

Serves 6–8

Above: A dusting with icing (confectioners') sugar adds an attractive topping to Almond and Apricot Cake.
Left: A slice of cake being served with cream.

Almond and Apricot Cake

This is delicious served at room temperature with a little cream or yoghurt.

2½ cups milk	4 tablespoons slivered almonds
4 tablespoons sugar	15 g/½ oz/1 tablespoon butter
1 cup arborio rice	Grated peel of 1 lemon
3 eggs	1 teaspoon ground cinnamon
3 tablespoons mixed peel	1 teaspoon ground cardamom
60 g/2 oz/½ cup dried apricots, chopped	Icing (confectioners') sugar, to decorate

Put the milk, sugar and rice in a saucepan and bring to the boil. Stir, cover, lower the heat and cook for 15 minutes or until the rice is almost cooked. Cool.

Beat the eggs in a bowl and stir in the mixed peel, apricots, almonds, butter, lemon peel, cinnamon and cardamom. Stir the rice mixture into this thoroughly.

Butter a 20 cm/8 inch round cake tin and pour in the rice mixture. Bake in a preheated oven at 180°C/350°F/gas 4 for 30 minutes or until the top is brown. Dust with sifted icing sugar.
Serves 6–8

Glossary

Al dente: An Italian word referring to the texture of food—almost cooked, but remaining just a little firm. Italians like to eat their pasta, rice and vegetables this way.

Blanch: Immerse food briefly in boiling water to soften it or to remove skin.

Bouquet garni: A combination of fresh bay leaf, thyme and parsley tied with string or, if dried, tied up in a muslin (cheesecloth) bag. Used to flavour soups, casseroles and braises, stocks, poached and boiled dishes and sauces.

Dice: Cut vegetables into small cubes about 1 cm/⅜ inch.

Jointed: Cut up chicken into serving pieces, either before or after cooking (p. 28).

Marinate: Soak raw ingredients in a liquid to flavour them and to make them more tender, using wine, oil, vinegar, lemon juice, herbs and spices.

Olive oil: Use the finest quality for salads. The first cold pressing of the olives is the extra virgin oil and the highest quality flavour. Every pressing after that gives lower and lower standards of oil. The earlier the pressing, the better the flavour.

Parmesan cheese: Parmigiano-reggiano, the famous hard grating cheese from Italy. Used to flavour soups and pasta. Best to buy in a wedge and grate freshly as needed.

Preheated oven: Turn on the oven before beginning the recipe so it will have reached the desired temperature when you require it. Most ovens will take about 15 minutes to heat.

Purée: Render vegetables into pulp either by putting them through a food processor, blender, mouli or pushing them through a sieve (strainer).

Sauté: French for 'to jump', it means briskly cook in a small quantity of very hot oil, or a mixture of oil and butter, in a large frying pan (skillet). The food is just browned or cooked through.

Simmer: Keep a liquid just below boiling point so that it 'shivers'.

Skim: Remove the scum from a liquid after it comes to the boil, usually with a large spoon or a flat sieve (strainer).

Stoned (pitted) olives: Olives with the stone removed. There are special pieces of kitchen equipment for removing the stones, otherwise use a small knife to prise the olive open to remove the stone.

Vinegar: Produced by acetic fermentation in wine or cider, it can also be flavoured by herbs, spices, shallots and garlic or raspberries. Balsamic vinegar is an aged vinegar (10–50 years) with a wonderful, delicate flavour.